Herkimer County
Community College Library
Herkimer, New York
13350

1. Books may be kept for three weeks and may be renewed once, except when otherwise noted.

2. Reference books, such as dictionaries and encyclopedias are to be used only in the Library.

3. A fine is charged for each day a book is not returned according to the above rule.

4. All injuries to books beyond reasonable wear and all losses shall be made good to the satisfaction of the Librarian.

5. Each borrower is held responsible for all books drawn on his card and for all fines accruing on the same.

DEMCO

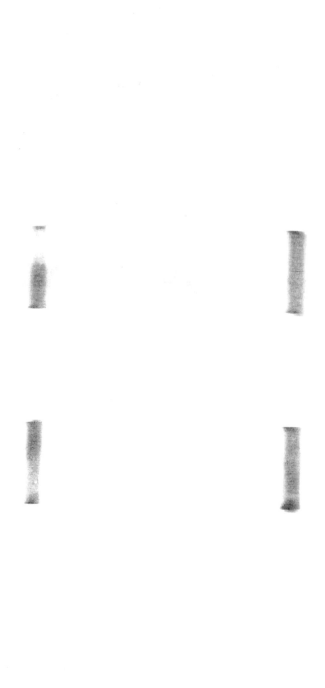

THE
FOUNDATIONS OF
AESTHETICS

Frontispiece

See page 75

i. a. richards
c. k. ogden
james wood

the
foundations
of aesthetics

HASKELL HOUSE PUBLISHERS LTD.
Publishers of Scarce Scholarly Books
NEW YORK. N. Y. 10012
1974

HASKELL HOUSE PUBLISHERS Ltd.

Publishers of Scarce Scholarly Books

280 LAFAYETTE STREET

NEW YORK, N. Y. 10012

Library of Congress Cataloging in Publication Data

Ogden, Charles Kay, 1889-1957.
  The foundations of aesthetics.

  Reprint of the 1925 ed. published by Lear Publishers,
New York.
  Richards' and Ogden's names in reverse order in
1922 London ed.
  1. Aesthetics. I. Richards, Ivor Armstrong,
1893-   joint author. II. Wood, James Edward
Hathorn, joint author. III. Title.
BH201.05 1974   111.8'5   74-1364
ISBN 0-8383-2046-5

PREFACE TO THE SECOND EDITION

THE reprinting of these pages allows us an opportunity of indicating any alterations of view which might seem desirable. But the reception accorded to the book, even in the short time which has elapsed since the first impression appeared, has strengthened our conviction of its serviceableness ; and were we writing to-day neither the general position, nor the particular mode of exposition would be changed. The advantages of a brief laconic argument are appreciated by those who prefer active rather than passive participation.

Some of the problems here treated are more fully dealt with in other works by the same authors. On the Verbal Problem, *The Meaning of Meaning,** on the Theory of Value, *The Principles of Literary Criticism,** and on general Psychological Principles, *The A.B.C. of Psychology,*† may be consulted, while additional comment on the technique of the Artist will be found in *Colour Harmony.**

*London, Kegan Paul; New York, Harcourt, Brace.

†New York, Harpers; London, Cambridge Magazine.

ORIGINAL PREFACE

INTEREST in questions of Aesthetics has been greatly stimulated during the past few years both by a wider knowledge of non-European—particularly of Eastern and primitive—Art, and by the rapid development of Psychology as a science. Traditional methods of approach equally with vague philosophical speculations have been found inadequate, and the need for a new orientation is evident to most students of recent theoretical publications.

In the following pages an attempt is made to present in a condensed form the greater part of accredited opinion on the subject, and to relate the views thus presented to the main positions from which the theory of art-criticism may proceed. It is hoped that in this way it will serve either as an introduction to those who from a literary point of view or as practical artists are interested in the problems which divergences of aesthetic judgments raise, or as a text-books for students of the Theory of Criticism itself. The discussion therefore follows a rather unusual course, its aim being not to bring theories into opposition with one another, but by distinguishing them to allow to each its separate sphere of validity. If verbal conflicts are avoided, there will be seen to be many possible theories of Beauty, not one only, the understanding of which may help in the appreciation of Art.

The attitude of tolerance which this treatment implies may require a corresponding effort on the part of the reader. Much that on first inspection appears inconclusive or obscure, will, it is hoped, be better understood as the partial separation of the fields dealt with by the different theories is more clearly realised. The theory of Synaesthesis with which our discussion ends is, however, in a special position. As an explanation of the aesthetic experiences described by many of the greatest and most sensitive artists and critics of the past, it may perhaps be regarded as the theory of Beauty *par excellence*.

The appreciation of Beauty, whether in Painting, Music or Poetry or in everyday experience, cannot but be developed by a clearer knowledge of what it is and where it may be looked for, and an acquaintance with the opinions of artists and philosophers on this subject will assist those who wish to increase their powers of discrimination and thereby to lay the foundations of a genuine and at the same time personal taste. It should also be noted that by uniting varied qualifications the authors have been enabled to treat the subject in a more catholic fashion than is usual, and to make it less likely that any important aspect of interest to the general reader has been overlooked.

It remains to add a brief reference to the quotations and the reproductions. When no other object is expressly stated, quotations provide a concrete illustration of some critical point discussed in the passage immediately preceding, and are therefore not to be regarded as additional commentary. They are intended mainly as a constant reminder of what the discussion is about, and are given as fully as space permits in order that the reader may have this opportunity of escaping from the scientific language of the argument. And as regards the reproductions, most of which have been specially made for the purpose,* it is hardly necessary to add that they are not put forward as the " Best pictures," nor are they typical in all cases of their period or place of origin. Each, however, adequately illustrates one *or more* of the theories discussed, and it will be obvious that all of them are works of high rank.

*For permission to photograph the Hogarth (Plate VIII) we have to thank the Directors of the Foundling Hospital. Plates II, III and XV are the copyright of the Folkwang Verlag, Hagen, i.W., Plate IV of Messrs. Braun & Co., and Plate VII of the International Portrait Service. The Chinese painting on silk (Plate XIV) is darkened with age and this has made its adequate reproduction a matter of considerable difficulty. In the Frontispiece and Plates VI, IX, and XIV, details only are given, as the presentation of the entire picture on so small a scale would have rendered appreciation impossible. We are indebted to Mr. C. H. Hsu for writing the Chinese characters which signify the Doctrine of Equilibrium and Harmony.

CONTENTS

9

LIST OF ILLUSTRATIONS

11

Plate 1.

See page 75.

MY *master the celebrated Chang says:
"Having no leanings is called Chung, admitting of no change is called Yung. By Chung is denoted Equilibrium; Yung is the fixed principle regulating everything under heaven."*

13

THE FOUNDATIONS OF AESTHETICS

What heaven has ordained is man's Nature; an accordance with this is the Path; the regulation of it is Instruction.

There is nothing more visible than what is secret—nothing more manifest than what is minute. The superior man is careful: he is but one.

When anger, sorrow, joy, pleasure are in being but are not manifested, the mind may be said to be in a state of Equilibrium; when the feelings are stirred and co-operate in due degree the mind may be said to be in a state of Harmony. Equilibrium is the great principle.

If both Equilibrium and Harmony exist everything will occupy its proper place and all things will be nourished and flourish.

From the Chung Yung
The Doctrine of Equilibrium and Harmony.

THE
FOUNDATIONS OF AESTHETICS

Many intelligent people give up aesthetic speculation and take no interest in discussions about the nature or object of Art, because they feel that there is little likelihood of arriving at any definite conclusion. Authorities appear to differ so widely in their judgments as to which things are beautiful, and when they do agree there is no means of knowing *what* they are agreeing about.

What in fact do they mean by Beauty? Prof. Bosanquet and Dr. Santayana, Signor Croce and Clive Bell, not to mention Ruskin and Tolstoi, each in his own way dogmatic, enthusiastic and voluminous, each leaves his conclusions equally uncorrelated with those of his predecessors. And the judgments of experts on one another are no less at variance. But if there is no reason to suppose that people are talking about the same thing, a lack of correlation in their remarks need not cause surprise. We assume too readily that similar language involves similar thoughts and similar things thought of. Yet why should there be only one subject of investigation which has been called Aesthetics ? Why not several fields to be separately investigated, whether they are found to be connected or not? Even a Man of Letters, given time, should see that if we say with the poet:

" 'Beauty is Truth, Truth Beauty'—that is all
　　Ye know on earth, and all ye need to know."

we need not be talking about the same thing as the author who says :

　　" The hide of the rhinoceros may be admired for its fitness ; but as it scarcely indicates vitality, it is deemed less beautiful than a skin which exhibits mutable effects of muscular elasticity."

What reason is there to suppose that one aesthetic doctrine can be framed to include all the valuable kinds of what is called Literature :—

" All tongues speak of him, and the bleared
　　sights
Are spectacled to see him, your prattling nurse
Into a rapture lets her baby cry
While she chats him : the kitchen malkin pins
Her richest lockram 'bout her reechy neck
Clamb'ring the walls to eye him."

To this satire may be opposed the unsubstantial music of the following passage, yet both must take a high place in any account of literary values :—

" Such a soft floating witchery of sound
As twilight Elphins make, when they at eve
Voyage on gentle gales from Fairyland,
Where Melodies round honey-dropping flowers,
Footless and wild, like birds of Paradise,
Nor pause, nor perch, hovering on untam'd
     wing ! "

No one explanation seems sufficient to cover such a wide difference. It is not surprising therefore that aesthetic theories are equally different. Let us nevertheless attempt to make a classification.

B

I.

AESTHETIC EXPERIENCES

Whenever we have any experience which might be called 'aesthetic,' that is whenever we are enjoying, contemplating, admiring or appreciating an object, there are plainly different parts of the situation on which emphasis can be laid. As we select one or other of these so we shall develop one or other of the main aesthetic doctrines. In this choice we shall, in fact, be deciding which of the main Types of Definition* we are employing. Thus we may begin with the object itself ; or with other things such as Nature, Genius, Perfection, The Ideal, or Truth, to which it is related ; or with its effects upon us. We may begin where we please, the important thing being that we should know and make clear which of these approaches it is that we are taking, for the objects with which we come to deal, the referents to which we refer, if we enter one field will not as a rule be the same as those in another. Few persons will be equally interested in all, but some acquaintance with them will at least make the interests of other

* A full account of these will be found in Chapter V. of *The Meaning of Meaning* (Kegan Paul, 1922) by the same authors.

people more intelligible, and discussion more profitable. Differences of opinion and differences of interest in these matters are closely interconnected, but any attempt at a general synthesis, premature perhaps at present, must begin by disentangling them. A third quotation essentially unlike either of those already given above may help to make this quite clear:—

"By the waters of Babylon
We sat down and wept :
When we remembered thee, O Sion.

As for our harps, we hanged them up :
Upon the trees that are therein.

For they that led us away captive required
    of us then a song,
And melody in our heaviness :
Sing us one of the songs of Sion.

How shall we sing the Lord's song:
In a strange land ?

If I forget thee, O Jerusalem :
Let my right hand forget her cunning.

If I do not remember thee,
Let my tongue cleave to the roof of my
    mouth :
Yea, if I prefer not Jerusalem in my mirth.

Remember the Children of Edom, O Lord,
In the day of Jerusalem :
How they said, Down with it, down with it,
Even to the ground.

O daughter of Babylon, wasted with misery :
Yea, happy shall he be that rewardeth thee,
As thou hast served us.

Blessed shall he be that taketh thy children :
    and throweth them
Against the stones."

We have then to make plain the method of Definition which we are employing. The range of useful methods is shown in the following table of definitions, most of which represent traditional doctrines, while others, not before emphasised, render the treatment approximately complete.

It should be borne in mind throughout this volume that anything judged to be beautiful is either a work of art or a natural object. A work of art may clearly *be regarded* in both ways, but not simultaneously. When we regard it as a work of art we take the attitude of the contemplator, our attitude, that is to say, is modified by the preceding activity of another mind ; but when we look at it as a natural object (as we *may* do in painting a cathedral) we take the attitude of an artist, that is to say, we make our own selection.

THE SENSES OF BEAUTY

A
    I *Anything is beautiful — which possesses the simple quality of Beauty.*

    II *Anything is beautiful — which has a specified Form.*

B {

III *Anything is beautiful—which is an imitation of Nature.*

IV *Anything is beautiful—which results from successful exploitation of a Medium.*

V *Anything is beautiful—which is the work of Genius.*

VI *Anything is beautiful—which reveals (1) Truth, (2) the Spirit of Nature, (3) the Ideal, (4) the Universal, (5) the Typical.*

VII *Anything is beautiful—which produces Illusion.*

VIII *Anything is beautiful—which leads to desirable Social effects.*

IX *Anything is beautiful—which is an Expression.*

C {

X *Anything is beautiful—which causes Pleasure.*

XI *Anything is beautiful—which excites Emotions.*

XII *Anything is beautiful—which promotes a Specific emotion.*

XIII *Anything is beautiful—which involves the processes of Empathy.*

XIV *Anything is beautiful—which heightens Vitality.*

XV *Anything is beautiful—which brings us into touch with exceptional Personalities.*

XVI *Anything is beautiful—which conduces to Synaesthesis*

The fields reached by these various approaches can all be cultivated and most of them are associated with well known names in the Philosophy of Art.*

Let us, however, suppose that we have selected one of these fields and cultivated it to the best of our ability ; for what reasons was it selected rather than some other ? For if we approach the subject in the spirit of a visitor to the Zoo, who, knowing that all the creatures in a certain enclosure are ' reptiles,' seeks for the common property which distinguishes them as a group from the fish in the Aquarium, mistakes may be made. We enter, for example, the Fitzwilliam Museum, and, assuming that all the objects there collected are beautiful, attempt similarly to establish some common property. A little consideration of how they came there might have raised serious doubts ; but if, after the manner of many aestheticians, we persist, we may even make our discovery of some relevant common property appear plausible.

Anyone, however, who, after a study of these and similar objects, wished to know why he should prefer one to another would find himself confronted by the possibilities we have set forth in our list.

* As this discussion is throughout concerned with the theory of Beauty, we are not called upon to examine the various senses in which the word Art has also been used. Thus when we refer to Art in connection with e.g., Imitation, we are referring to beauty in anything that has generally been called Art as opposed to Nature.

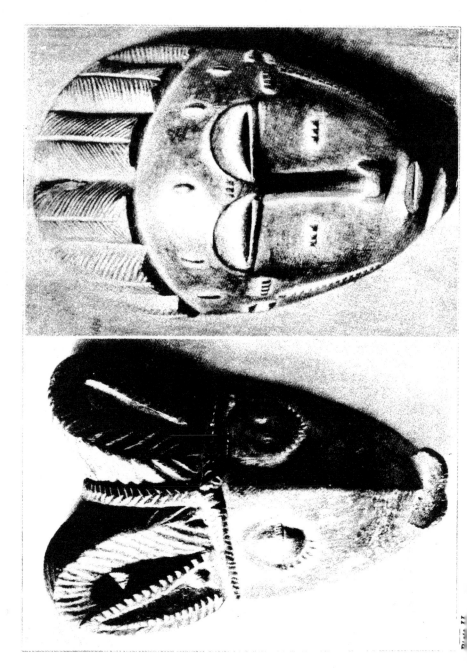

Plate II

II.

BEAUTY AS INTRINSIC

If the reader decide to admit **I** simple aesthetic properties,* such as beauty, loveliness, grandeur and prettiness, and supposes that things have these properties as they have redness or temperature, he has the dictionary on his side, but gets no further enlightenment as to the nature of his experiences. Such an aesthetic, though capable of much elegant internal development, as, for example, the pos-

---

*As an example of an able and considered statement of the case for an intrinsic quality we may refer to pp. 127-144 of Professor John Laird's *Study in Realism.* " Human actions," concludes Professor Laird, " are good or bad in a moral sense, a value or its opposite belongs to them in the same sense as redness belongs to a cherry. For similar reasons the values of beauty or its opposite belong to certain things in certain connecticns, just as objectively as any other qualities." Sculpture such as that shewn in Plate II, might lead theorists to conclusions of this kind.

For a view of the second type (*i.e.*, objective beauty as certain relations, etc., in a physical complex), with which, as we shall see, Mr. Roger Fry toys in his remarks about necessary relations, reference may be made to the contention by Professor Kirschman in the University of Toronto Psychological Studies : " A picture is a surface (a part of our field of vision), consisting of smaller surfaces which differ in space relation (extension, shape, arrangement), light quality (colour-tone and saturation), light intensity. All properties which the picture as a whole or in its parts possess, must be reducible to qualities or relations of these small surfaces. Consequently, any quality attributed to the work of art or its parts must be capable of being expressed in terms of these five or six variables."

tulation of a special Sense of Beauty, has no connections with any other aspects of the Universe. Beauty becomes an ultimate un-analysable idea, and no criticism or discussion is possible. Such a view gains support from the existence of many works whose artistic value it has been difficult to explain by current theories (Plate III), or which have not generally been regarded as works of Art—*e.g.*, aeroplanes, etc. If, on the other hand, he does not allow such properties and considers that what he is preferring is **II** some arrangement of physical features, he is committed to the view that one arrangement of physical features can be *in itself* preferable to (more valuable than) another. It is at least doubtful whether there is any sense in speaking of a preference for (the value of) things other than mental states or experiences. When people say they prefer coffee to tea, they will, if questioned, generally admit that it is either one flavour which they prefer to another, or one set of mental effects ; and if they tasted neither, nor had effects from either, the two potations would be indifferent. Our inquirer will, on these grounds, take a psychological view, unless he is attracted by one of the doctrines comprised under group B.

Plate III.   See page 24

III.

IMITATION

Among these we find what is, perhaps, the most popular view that has ever been held, the view namely **III** that art is essentially Imitation, and that a picture or a poem is beautiful in proportion as what it successfully imitates or describes is beautiful.

" The artist wrought this loved Guitar,
  And taught it justly to reply,
  To all who question skilfully,
  In language gentle as its own,
  Whispering in enamoured tone
  Sweet oracles of woods and dells,
  And summer winds in sylvan cells ;
  For it had learnt all harmonies
  Of the plains and of the skies,
  Of the forests and the mountains,
  And the many voiced fountains ;
  The clearest echoes of the hills,
  The softest notes of falling rills,
  The melodies of birds and bees,
  The murmuring of summer seas,
  And pattering rain and breathing dew,
  And airs of evening ; and it knew
  That seldom-heard mysterious sound,
  Which, driven in its diurnal round,
  As it floats through boundless day,
  Our world enkindles on its way."

The implication that the problem of the beautiful as such would merely have been shifted into the realm of nature is generally concealed by a use of language which seems to place the beauty in the imitation itself (*cf.* Plate IV). Aristotle combines this view with the pleasure doctrine, urging that there is a special pleasure in recognition. With the advent of the camera, however, the unique function of the artist was challenged, and at the same time theological considerations no longer allowed a certain merit to every picture *qua* replica of God's handiwork. To-day the esteem felt for mimicry and imitation is perceptibly dwindling.

In this connection it may be mentioned that, as with Eastlake's elephant *infra*, those who regard sunsets, peacocks, roses, river-girls and racehorses as specially beautiful are generally making what Lalo has described as " an implicit, confused or instinctive judgment of the more or less normal, healthy and typical or more or less powerful and highly developed character of a being or object of a given kind." As is well known, such judgments are readily confused with other ascriptions of beauty.

Plate IV.

See page 26

IV.

THE MEDIUM

It is, however, interesting to consider what may be meant by the dictum of the studios that things should be drawn " as they really look," and concurrently by Mr. Clive Bell's contention that representation of any kind is always irrelevant in Art. Representation involves two things, what is represented and a Medium. Let us first consider the general problem of the medium and its use, approaching the question through the three divisions of our list, from each of which we naturally arrive at different conclusions.

For doctrines of Group A the question is without interest; how medium and use are connected in a work will not for them be necessarily relevant. The work has beauty or has not beauty in the one case, in the other it either is of a certain physical form or it is not.

With doctrines of Group B the case is much the same. An Imitationist pure would be forced to the position that the more like the medium is to the matter of the object represented, the better. The pure theory of Imitation, however, is uncommon, being usually compounded either with Revelatory or with Psychological Doctrines. Revelatory theorists favour somewhat the view that the less like the two are the better, but are not greatly concerned and leave the matter to the Psychologists. Social Moralists only intervene in disguise, and Expressionists hold for a mystic undiscussable relation of fitness.

We are thus left with C, the Psychological Theories. Of these the pleasure view tends to come into conflict with the others. There are certain suitabilities which connect media with their employment in the following fashion: Every medium has as a material its own peculiar effect upon our impulses. Thus our feelings towards clay and iron, towards the organ and the piano, towards colloquial and ceremonial speech are entirely different. Now upon all hands it is agreed, that these peculiar impulses must not be neglected. Those who maintain the pleasure view tend, however, to give them a special place by holding that the proper connection between medium and employment is that the employment must give to these impulses as much free play as possible on the ground that the free play of any impulse is pleasurable. The artist, they say, must respect the character of his medium and exploit it (Plate V). It is even common to find the view maintained **IV** that Art *is* the exploitation of the Medium.*

Those who hold the other psychological doctrines differ in refusing to allow so simple a connection such importance. While not denying that it is more natural to do certain things with one medium and other things with another they yet agree in laying no particular stress on the gratification of this group of impulses. They point out that there are many other impulses involved and hold that the emotion, vitality, empathy or equilibrium which they desiderate, may require adjustments between the sets of impulses due to the medium and to its use, very different from mere mutual accommodation.

" Apter they are through the eagerness of their affection, that maketh them, which way soever they take, diligent in drawing their husbands, children, servants, friends and allies the same way ; apter through that natural inclination unto pity, which breedeth in them a greater readiness than in men to be bountiful towards their preachers who suffer want ; apter through sundry opportunities which they have to procure encouragement for their brethren ; finally, apter through a singular delight which they take in giving very large and

---

* *Cf.* Mr. Marriott in the recent Oxford Symposium on "Mind and Medium in Art," *B. J. Psych*, xi. 1 ("Art is primarily the characteristic use of tools and materials," etc.).

particular intelligence how all nearabout them stand affected as concerning the same cause."

Although the medium and its use are here adapted to one another, this accordance is not so simple as a mere mutual accommodation, and conversely this last may be present in perfection in works of no merit whatever.

What, however, is at the root of the advice given to young artists to forget what they think things look like and draw them as they actually see them, is best explicable from our ways of recognising what we see. The exigencies of every day life accustom us to selecting only those aspects of experience which have a permanent and practical use. We normally react to our surroundings in ways which are labelled and classified in language, as stereotyped names. Thus grass is green or death is the end of life. In order, however, to react freely before a subject we must endeavour to be as little influenced by our habitual selections and attitudes as possible,—and this in the interest of representation itself. Death is the end of life—

"Or is it only a sweet slumber
    Stealing o'er sensation,
    Which the breath of roseate morning
    Chaseth into darkness ? "

What has to be reproduced is what is affecting the artist and nothing else, nothing

See page 31

Plate VI.

dragged from some other context or irrelevant experience. Thus men are often seen as though they had one leg, the other being in fact either invisible or irrelevant. But if any memory or convention or assumption that men must have two legs leads us to draw in a couple of lower limbs his will be actually to the detriment of our representation. We must not, however, say with Mr. Clive Bell that the artist should "bring nothing from life," no acquaintance with its emotions or its experiences.* This is not only to demand an impossibility, but also arbitrarily and unnecessarily to restrict the field of aesthetic experience. What Mr. Clive Bell perhaps desires to recommend is the attitude above described, but (unfortunately for his view) in every visual act we unavoidably bring to bear much of our past experience. The artist selects in virtue of the impulses which his past life has developed in him. When we look at his work we shall in many cases miss much that is essential unless we are able to react with similar impulses (Plate VI). To do so is necessarily to involve our past life. If with Mr. Bell we regard as irrelevant everything except colour, line and

---

* Delacroix, *Journal* Vol. III, p. 97, raises a similar question, which presents no difficulties—"Si nous sommes faits pour trouver dans cette créature qui nous charme le genre d'attrait propre à nous captiver, comment expliquer que ces mêmes traits, ces mêmes grâces particulières, pourront nous laisser froids, quand nous les trouverons exprimées dans les tableaux ou les statues."

form, we may lessen the danger of undesirable associations, but at the price of missing a vital element in the work of art. The dispute is a little academic, because, as remarked above, this attitude could never be achieved by man, bird or beast. In most painting the representational element in its proper place has its own important function. In poetry this is more obvious.

"We twa hae run about the braes,
　And pou'd the gowans fine ;
But we've wander'd mony a weary fitt,
　Sin auld lang syne.

We twa hae paidl'd in the burn,
　Frae morning sun till dine ;
But seas between us braid hae roar'd
　Sin auld lang syne."

While emphasing the influence of past experience, we need not go so far as Lafcadio Hearn, who says: "When there is perceived some objective comeliness faintly corresponding to certain outlines of the inherited ideal, at once a wave of emotion ancestral bathes the long darkened image . . . the sense-reflection of the living objective becomes temporarily blended with the subjective phantasm,—with the beautiful luminous ghost made of centillions of memories . . . And so the Riddle resolves itself as Memory"* Such 'organic memory' is however, equally involved (cf. p. 68 infra) in all our experience whether of Beauty or not.

*Exotics and Retrospectives, pp. 202, 206.

V.

GENIUS

Another doctrine of Group B, concerns **V** Genius. The distinction between classes of objects in virtue of their origin is well-known in many scientific fields ; and common objects also are often identified by this means. Thus when we refer to Madeira, we have in view certain wines grouped together as coming from that source ; and so it has been supposed that we know a work of art or recognise beauty as the creation of a certain type of man.

Thus we find Professor Külpe in a lengthy discussion of "The Conception and Classification of Art" (University of Toronto Studies, Vol. 2, 1907) taking as his starting point the definition, "Art is the product of genius—according to Kant and Schopenhauer," and objecting that genius produces scientific work as well, and that in the productions of works of art, "more modest talent than genius is also acknow-

C

33

ledged." Light on the nature of genius from this point of view is thrown by doctrines which appear in Bergsonian literature.*

* Thus in Ruge's *Henri Bergson: an Account of his Life and Philosophy*, we read, " The more we are entangled in living the less truly we are able to see. . . . We hardly see the object itself ; we are content to know the class to which it belongs. We are content ; but from time to time by happy chance men are born who are not bound to the treadmill of practical life. When they see a thing they look at it for itself ; and according to circumstances become painters or sculptors, musicians or poets. What the artist gives us is, in short, a more direct vision of reality. . . . Nature thus at long intervals, and as though unawares, reveals reality to certain privileged beings." If from phraseology such as this we are led to the not unnatural conclusion that Art is whatever certain privileged beings produce, we have a means of recognising art when we have decided who amongst us are privileged and who suffering from illusions ; and the controversy is shifted into the realms of social psychology.

> " I hae a wife o' my ain
>   I'll partake wi naebody,
> I'll tak' cuckold frae nain,
>   I'll gie cuckold to naebody.
>
> I hae a penny to spend,
>   There—thanks to naebody ;
> I hae naething to lend,
>   I'll borrow frae naebody.
>
> I am naebody's lord,
>   I'll be slave to naebody ;
> I hae a quid braid sword,
>   I'll tak dunts frae naebody.
>
> I'll be merry and free,
>   I'll be sad for naebody ;
> Naebody cares for me,
>   I care for naebody."

34

VI.

TRUTH

The general method employed in this enquiry is nowhere more valuable than in the discussion of **VI** Revelation. By its aid we may free ourselves in part from the apparent conflicts which the phonetic and graphic overlaps of distinct vocabularies (*i.e.* the use of the same terms to mean different things) occasion. In all revelatory doctrines, we are concerned in one sense or another with Truth. The relevant definitions of truth are at least as varied as those of Beauty. They cannot be adequately discussed here ; one such set of opinions providing sufficient mental exercise for one occasion, but a few broad distinctions may be noted without overstraining the attention.

Thus when Aristotle suggests that the artist besides imitating should also preserve the type and at the same time ennoble it his suggestion may be taken in many ways. Eastlake, for instance, understands that, " The elephant with his objectionable legs and inexpressive hide, may still be supposed to be a very normal specimen and so worthy of imitation by the artist." which is one way of interpreting ' the universal,' namely as the typical. And Rymer in objecting to Shakespeare's Iago : " He would pass upon us a close, dissembling, false, insinuating rascal, instead of an open-hearted, frank, plain-dealing Souldier, a character constantly worn by them for some thousands of years in the World," provides another interpretation namely as the conventional. Thirdly, Croce remarks of the view that art is imitation, "Now truth has been maintained or at least shadowed with these words, now error. More frequently, nothing definite has been thought. One of the legitimate scientific meanings occurs when imitation is understood as representation or intuition of nature, a form of knowledge [*cf.* Plate VII]. And when this meaning has been understood, by placing in greater relief the spiritual character of the process, the other proposition becomes also legitimate ; namely that art is the idealisation or idealising imitation of nature."

" Hark, hark ! the lark at heaven's gate sings,
    And Phœbus 'gins arise,
  His steeds to water at those springs
    On chaliced flowers that lies."

Plate VII.

See page 36

Yet other variants may be found in Matthew Arnold for whom commerce with certain forms of art seemed " to make those who constantly practised it . . . like persons who have had a very weighty and impressive experience : more truly than others under the empire of facts, and more independent of the language current among those with whom they live " ; and in Coleridge " The artist must imitate that which is within the thing, that which is active through form and figure, and discourses to us by symbols,—the Naturgeist, or spirit of nature," elsewhere defining beauty as " the subjection of matter to spirit so as to be transformed into a symbol, in and through which the spirit reveals itself."

MYSTICISM

It is plain that such different views as these require separate handling. Matthew Arnold's observation may be postponed until we discuss the doctrine of equilibrium within which it will find both a place and an explanation. Let us here consider the only other of these five views which requires attention, namely that of Coleridge. Having been stated as a mystical view, it can evidently only appeal in this form to those who adopt the special attitudes involved.

One natural statement of the mystical doctrine involved would be as follows. A certain emotion has occurred in the contemplation of a work of art or of nature, which represents or symbolises either a special selection, or else in the supreme case the whole of, the past experience of the individual. It enables us to think of a complete range of experience, and this range is regarded as a datum upon a different level from any of the data provided by portions of that range, and capable of giving knowledge as to the nature of the universe which the partial data of everyday experience do not readily yield.

Those to whom such an idea appears extravagant will explain the peculiar character of the emotions in question by saying perhaps that they are associated with unrecalled events in past experience.

The view of the world of art as a better world into which we may escape from the drabness and dulness of the present has close affinities with some kinds of idealisation.

"Then let the winds howl on! their harmony
Shall henceforth be my music, and the night
The sound shall temper with the owlets' cry,
As I now hear them in the fading light
Dim o'er the bird of darkness' native site,
Answer each other on the Palatine,
With their large eyes, all glistening grey and
    bright,
And sailing pinions.   Upon such a shrine
What are our petty griefs?—let me not num-
    ber mine."

VII.

ILLUSION

If, however, **VII** Illusion is brought forward as the end of art we have a view which can be discussed on its own merits. Those who admire imitation are already on the way to such a view, and a picture which is merely regarded as a substitute for what might actually be seen is producing an illusion. It is only a further step to demand that the illusion shall be one of a more exciting, more inaccessible, or more congenial environment than the ordinary. On this theory Art is "the quickest way out of Manchester"; and one can " lose oneself in a novel," or " forget one's troubles at the play " as easily as in drink.

This pre-occupation with art as a means of escape is probably the cause of the public's taking so little interest in any but certain forms of representative art. An elaborate attempt has been made by Konrad Lange to justify this theory of art on the ground that man has an instinct to self-deception, which the artist satisfies; the essence of aesthetic appreciation being conscious self - deception. To the satirist or misanthrope such a theory often makes an appeal.

VIII.

SOCIAL EFFECTS

We may next consider the peculiar group of **VIII** Uplift doctrines which have emerged from the industrious homes of the late Victorian moralists. Mr. John Ruskin, in spite of his real taste, maintained in his *Oxford Lectures* that Fine Art has only three functions —Enforcing the religious sentiments of men, Perfecting their ethical state, and Doing them material service (Plate VIII). The two last of these were also stressed by William Morris, and the two first by Tolstoi; it is, however, curious that Tolstoi's *What is Art?* shews no evidence of acquaintance with the work of Ruskin.

Tolstoi's insistence that great art must appeal to mankind in general is not necessarily connected with his moralistic and less valuable contentions; and advocates of a People's Theatre (*cf.* Romain Rolland's criteria) often seem to confuse the issue. From the side of Uplift, on the other hand, Professor W. R. Lethaby for instance in the *Hibbert Journal*, considers that "Art is best conceived as beneficent Labour which blesses

See page 40

both him who gives and him who receives. Beauty is its evidence. Beauty is virtue in being." Or as Mr. Middleton Murry has it, in his *Evolution of an Intellectual* (p. 55), the artist is he who " by the compelling rhythm of his own progress becomes more and more a vehicle of the spirit which is for ever wrestling with its own materiality, . . . he but guides the world to the achievement of its own design. He penetrates and seeks to identify himself with this timeless progress, in order that he may become as it were, the taproot of the spirit which is at work in the world he contem plates."

Finally Mr. Clutton-Brock in his *Essays on Art* (1919) hazards the definition that the beauty of art " is always produced by the effort to accomplish the impossible, and what the artist knows to be impossible. Art is the expression of a certain attitude towards reality, an attitude of wonder and value, a recognition of something greater than man ; and where that recognition is not, art dies."

We may compare and contrast the aristocratic attitude:—

"I see before me the Gladiator lie:
He leans upon his hand—his manly brow
Consents to death, but conquers agony,
And his droop'd head sinks gradually low—

And through his side the last drops, ebbing
   slow
From the red gash, fall heavy, one by one,
Like the first of a thunder-shower; and now
The arena swims around him: he is gone,
Ere ceased the inhuman shout which hail'd
   the wretch who won.

He heard it, but he heeded not—his eyes
Were with his heart, and that was far away."

Considered as a post-war phenomenon the
chief function of the revival of gratulation
and homiletic is presumably the promotion
of comfortable feeling in the hearts of men of
good will, and as such no doubt it has a certain value. Some of these formulations will
be observed to have affinities with revelatory
doctrines moralised* through modern Pro-
testant influence, and in this connexion may
best be regarded as still-born poems.

---

* *Cf.* Baudelaire *Curiosités Esthetiques* p. 327 ''Qu'ils moisson-
nent, qu'ils sèment, qu'ils fassent paître des vaches, qu'ils ton-
dent des animaux, ils ont toujours l'air de dire: Pauvres dés-
herités de ce monde, c'est pourtant nous qui le fécondent! Nous
accomplissons une mission, nous exerçons un sacerdoce' Au lieu
d extraire simplement la poésie naturelle de son sujet, M.
Millet veut a tout prix y ajouter quelque chose. Dans leur mono-
tone laideur, tous ces petits parias ont une pretention philoso-
phique, melancolique et raphaélesque. Ce malheur, dans la pein-
ture de M. Millet, gâte toutes les belles qualités qui attirent
tout d'abord le regard vers lui.''

IX.

EXPRESSIONISM

The most widely quoted formulation of the
IX Expressionist view of Art, is that of
Croce.

For certain readers this doctrine has a
peculiar glamour. Impressionable essayists,
who do not often meet with serious argumen-
tation in the course of their literary perusals,
and romantic persons who long for release
from the laborious process of discrimination,
are wont to find satisfaction in synthetic
philosophies of the spirit which achieve un-
hoped for unifications.

The keystone of Croce's method consists in
a skilful application of the Law of Identity
combined with a partial denial of the Law
of Contradiction. Thus when Intuition is
identified with Expression it may be asserted
that all intuitions are expressed without any
further necessity of proof. Then if Intuition-
expression be identified with Art, it follows
that all intuitions are works of art. Since
this process consists simply in the judicious
interchange of these strict synonyms the

irresistible sweep of Croce's argument meets with no obstacle, and a healthy air of vigorous ratiocination is engendered! But it may be objected that too many things become Art. To this Croce replies that this does not distress him because " no one has ever been able to indicate in what the something more consists . . . the limits of the expressions that are called Art as opposed to those that are vulgarly called ' not Art ' are empirical and impossible to define. If an epigram be art why not a single word ? "

Why not ? That is precisely the difficulty of every expressionist's view, and in being hypnotised by his doctrine into according aesthetic value to every single word (if a word is a work of art why not a comma, which expresses a distinct impression of a pause ?) Signor Croce himself invites us to attend the obsequies of expressionism. In fact the conclusion of the whole matter is the same as the beginning. Something happens which has been called Art, and which we too rightly call Art. This *is* Art.

As there is no reason to doubt his sincerity and as his literary, dramatic and historical writings are of such undoubted value, the most charitable explanation of this equivocation would be that Croce, preoccupied with the metaphysics of creative idealism, is endeavouring to say in speculative language something exceptionally obvious—for which he has attempted to create a personal vocabulary by exploiting the suggestive powers of accepted phrases.*

* With some confidence, then, it may be claimed, that Croce's English interpreters—such as Mr. Carritt, who states, on p. 281 of *The Theory of Beauty*, " a greater amount of truth is contained in Croce's *Estetica* than in any other philosophy of beauty that I have read," or the Reverend S. A. McDowall, who tells us on p. 18 of his *Beauty and the Beast* that " It has been left for Croce to formulate the first satisfactory concept of beauty " —are too easily satisfied by rhetorical solutions. Mr. Carritt, himself declares, " My reading of Croce has convinced me that the *expression* of *any* feeling is beautiful. . . . All beauty is the expression of what may be generally called emotion, and all such expression is beautiful ; " but almost in the same breath (p. 298) he goes on to admit that the only sort of ex- pression which can " strictly be called beautiful " is " a particular way in which at a given moment any individual expresses himself." We are left seeking further light on the particular way ; and even the most piously erotic will hardly be better satisfied with Mr. McDowall's improvement on his master— " Mainly out of the relationship of sex, spring music, art, literature. . . . Croce missed the goal because he did not perceive that the content of Reality is relationship. God is Love ; Reality is Love. Love is relationship. Beauty is the expression of an understanding of that relationship. Matter is beautiful because it is understood as the infinite activity of the spirit of love." " Matter," says Professor Eddington (*Space, Time and Gravitation*, p. 91), " is built of electrons or other nuclei," and if his theory is to be truly all-embracing Mr. McDowall should surely have said a word about the *libido* of the other nuclei, which are so infinitely active.

Eclecticism

Though it is less easy to extract a definite theory from the phraseology of Dr. Bosanquet than from that of Croce, he may probably be regarded as an expressionist, though he wisely differs from Croce in objecting to the use made of intuition. In the *History of Aesthetic* we are given the Definition of Beauty, viz. :—" That which has characteristic or individual expression for sense-perception or imagination, subject to the conditions of general or abstract expressiveness in the same medium." Whatever else may be extracted from these cryptic words we at least seem to be concerned primarily with an Expressionist theory, and in *Lectures on Aesthetic*, p. 33, we read " to say that the aesthetic attitude is an attitude of expression, contains, I believe, if rightly understood the whole truth of the matter." But unlike Croce, Bosanquet is always toying with the hedonic alternative—as if uncertain what part pleasure should play. Thus in the *Lectures*, he describes the aesthetic attitude as "preoccupation with a pleasant feeling, embodied

in an object which can be contemplated
. . . there is probably some trace of the
aesthetic attitude in almost all pleasant
feeling." We also learn (p. 103) that
pleasantness is not " a condition precedent
of beauty ; rather beauty is a condition
precedent of pleasantness," while elsewhere
(*History of Aesthetic*, p. 6), we note that
" things are not beautiful simply because
they give pleasure, but only in so far as they
give aesthetic pleasure." Our suspicions are
not allayed by the dictum " Beauty is feeling
become plastic," nor by this on the nature
of ugliness — " Suppose the beautiful silky
ear of a dachshund replacing the ear of a
beautiful human face. . . . Here we have
in principle, I think, a genuine case of ugliness " (*Lectures*, p. 102).

It is time, however, to turn from such
inconsequent, if suggestive, eclecticism* to
doctrines falling definitely within the psycho-

---

* We shall have occasion to note in relation to Empathy,
that it is easy for anyone who is not clear as to the question
he is endeavouring to answer to hover between several views
according to the interest or context with which he is momen-
tarily concerned. Thus one of the most informative of modern
aestheticians, whose death at the age of 33 prevented his attaining
that synthesis of which his learning and catholicity gave hope,
Marie Jean Guyau, speaks of Art (which in *L'Irréligion de l'avenir*
he regards as gradually taking the place of religion) for the
most part after the manner of George Eliot, who regarded it as
" a mode of amplifying experience and extending our contact
with our fellow-men beyond the bounds of our personal lot."
(Type XV). The highest end of art, we read, is " to produce
an aesthetic emotion of a social character," *de produire une
émotion esthétique d'un caractère social* (Type VIII) ; yet four

logical field* which includes the third main group of theories.

pages earlier (*L'art au point de vue sociologique* (p.17)), he gives us a definition which, quoted in isolation as Professor Ross quotes it in his *Social Control*, p. 258, might be taken for an adumbration of the doctrine of equilibrium to which we shall return later (Type XVI). Art then appears as " an *ensemble* of means of producing that general and harmonious stimulation of the conscious life which constitutes the sentiment of the beautiful." And when we turn to *L'esthétique contemporaine* for light on the difficulty, we get a third story (p. 77), this time purely hedonic. " Beauty can, as I think, be defined thus :— it is a perception or an action which stimulates in us life in all its three forms of sensibility, intelligence, and will at once, and produces pleasure by the rapid consciousness of this general stimulation . . . l'agréable est le fond même du beau." (Type X). When we add that Guyau found in play " l'art dramatique à son premier degré " (in reply to Grant Allen) and held that " Le type de l'émotion esthétique est l'emotion de l'amour. La beauté supérieure est la beauté feminine," it is hardly surprising to find M. Alfred Fouillée extracting from the works of his friend a Bergsonian doctrine of Art as " almost synonymous with universal sympathy," as that which " consiste a saisir et a rendre l'esprit des choses," by breaking down the barriers of the ego and " uniting the individual with the all, and every portion of time with the whole of duration." (Type VI).

* A subtle question is often raised here, namely, what it is which is to be called beautiful on these psychological views. Professor John Laird (*Realism*, p. 134), who, as we have noted, argues for the Intrinsic view (Type I), contends that Beauty is a predicate which " cannot hold of anything less than the whole complex thing-that-is-felt-with-delight "; and Professor Alexander, whose general attitude would seem to have been largely determined by the perusal of Bosanquet, remarks (*Space, Time, Deity*, Vol. II, p. 294) that " beauty belongs to the complex of mind and its object, to the beautiful object as expressed by the mind." Such formulations are clearly relevant ; and if we do not know whether we are applying the term beauty to the effect, to the cause, or to both together, purely verbal discussions, due to the Utraquistic Fallacy, will arise.

Psychological Views

The definition of Art in terms of psychological effect came particularly into prominence with the evolutionary theories of the seventies which occupied themselves chiefly in discovering the survival value in everything which had succeeded in making good its right to survive. The evolutionists of those days regarded pleasure as a feeling which could be correlated with physiological function, and since Art seemed a form of activity with little apparent utility it was considered wise to relate it closely to Play which (*vide* kittens) involved the very practical idea of Exercise. Various continuations were then possible. The first, adopted by Herbert Spencer, saw in Play*

---

* Though the relations of Art and Play are frequently discussed in the literature of Aesthetics (cf. *infra* p. 90), it has not been considered necessary to examine as independent contributions the views of those who put forward either a Play-theory or a Sex-theory of Art. The instincts of Sex, no less than those of Play, are no doubt connected in various ways with aesthetics, but few have as yet committed themselves to the absurdities involved in constructing a definition of Beauty on the basis of such connexions. We may recall, however, the opinion of Haydon (*Lectures on Painting and Design, 1846*, p.258), that the Beautiful " has its origin altogether in woman," and similar monstrosities may be found scattered throughout Phallic and Freudian literature. The fondness of writers like Mr. Edward Carpenter (*e.g.*, *The Art of Creation*, p. 188) for syntheses involving Beauty, Love and the World-soul (*cf.* the language of Mr. McDowall *supra*, p. 81) has helped to popularise such considerations.

D

and in Art a method of harmlessly expending superfluous energy. The faculties are as it were taken out for a trot lest they should atrophy or kick the stall down ; and since the pleasure we get from arrangements of sounds and colours appeared unconnected with any vital function, Spencer was able to regard Art and the contemplation of works of Art as a refined sort of game, an enjoyment *de luxe*, its special differentia being its absolute divorce from utility (Plate IX). This sort of treatment became known, and still is known, on the continent as the 'English aesthetic,'*

* " Aesthetic Pleasure," according to Grant Allen, p. 34," is the subjective concomitant of the normal amount of activity, not directly connected with life serving function, in the peripheral end organs of the cerebro-spinal nervous system "— the *passive* organs, whereas Play is the exercise of the *active* portion of our organism. " What Play is to the active faculties, Art and the Aesthetic Pleasures are to the passive."

Apart from the fact that Dancing is thus ruled out of the aesthetic field, the only further comment which need be made is the following extract from page 233 of Grant Allen's work, in which he voices a corollary of the pleasure-theory and the aesthetic requirements of his generation :—

" We demand that a painter should choose for his theme beautifully-shaped objects, such as human figures, male or female, in graceful attitudes, nude and exquisitely formed, with rounded limbs, or clothed in flowing drapery, Greek or Roman, Oriental or Florentine ; animals like the fawn, the panther, the Arab charger, the swan. and the butterfly ; mountain peaks, bossy hills, winding bays ; the cataract leaping in an arch from the crag ; Naples and Vesuvius and Niagara, the curved horizon of ocean, the thousand inlets of a highland loch ; graceful pottery, elegantly-moulded goblets, flagons, and vases, slender beakers and shapely chalices ; the domes and minarets of Stamboul. the sweeping arches of Tintern and Poitiers, the columns of Pæstum, the rounded tiers and galleries of the amphitheatre. On the other hand, the painter generally avoids (except for some special effect

Plate IX.

See page 50

partly because the Darwinian movement was already associated with these islands, and partly because the only English contribution to the theory of Aesthetics widely read on the continent in the century and a half which elapsed between Hogarth's *Analysis of Beauty* and the essays of Vernon Lee and Clive Bell is Grant Allen's *Physiological Aesthetics*.

of colour or contrast) lean, harsh, and angular limbs or features, constrained and graceless clothing, awkward postures and actions ; heavy, ungainly, or shapeless animal forms, such as the bear, the cart-horse, the goose, and the slug ; flat monotonous plains ; the still ocean unbroken by a winding shore or bluff headland, unrelieved by a ship with bellied sails or a tempest curling the breakers on the beach ; straight streets, plain rectangular houses, square windows, and flat façades destitute of arch or column, dome or portico."

To careful students of Burlington House it will come as no surprise to learn that in landscape painting " the choice of ' bits ' is one of the greatest tests of an artist's natural taste. Autumn and sunset are the chosen seasons of the painter as well as the poet." And finally " I have seen at least one painting of a throstle in a hawthorn bush, pouring forth its soul in open-mouthed delight, so that the very notes of its song trembled in one's ear "—or as Dr. Johnson might have said, " I have seen at least one painting of Scottish scenery in which, Sir, the road to England was so perspicuously delineated that the very traffic of Fleet Street roared in my delighted ear."

X.

PLEASURE

To take the most accomplished modern advocate of **X** the theory of Beauty as pleasure—" Beauty," says Dr. Santayana, is " pleasure regarded as a quality of a thing." All pleasures are intrinsic and positive values, and beauty is constituted by the objectification of pleasure (Plate X).

Once upon a time, the story runs, we thus objectified all our experiences, and thought that whatever happened to us had happened to things around us. But " modern philosophy has taught us to say the same thing of every element of the perceived world ; all are sensations ; and their grouping into objects imagined to be permanent and external is the work of certain habits of our intelligence."

In order to get a sense of Beauty therefore, we have to commit a " radically absurd fallacy." But since though recognising it as such, we can go on committing it, this doctrine is not quite self destructive, and those who are interested can examine the conditions under which we perform so curious and interesting an operation. We shall return to the question of objectification, or projection, in connection with the Einfühlung theory, and we shall also have occasion to notice that pleasure is assigned a subordinate place in

See page 52

Plate X.

most aesthetic doctrines, sometimes a necessary, more often a mere adventitious place. Meanwhile, there is no doubt that many people do use the term Beauty as a synonym for being the cause of pleasure, and the hedonist can be left to exploit his own field—the study of the things which please humanity—without interfering with others who have equally interesting work in hand.

The disadvantage of a pleasure view is that it offers us too restricted a vocabulary. We need fuller terms with which to describe the value of works of art.

" It is a beauteous evening, calm and free,
  The holy time is quiet as a nun
  Breathless with adoration ; the broad sun
  Is sinking down in its tranquillity ;
  The gentleness cf heaven broods o'er the
      sea.
  Listen ! the mighty being is awake,
  And doth with his eternal motion make
  A sound like thunder everlastingly.
  Dear child ! dear girl ! that walkest with me
      here,
  If thou appear untouched by solemn
      thought,
  Thy nature is not therefore less divine :
  Thou liest in Abraham's bosom all the year ;
  And worshipp'st at the temple's inner
      shrine,
  God being with thee when we know it
      not."

XI.

EMOTION

Let us next examine the claims of the Emotionalist. Works of art, it has been held, are those works which are produced under stress of emotion. The first consequence of such a view is that war poetry, the poetry of school-girls and not a little religious verse is thereby rendered an object of serious interest. If, instead, we chose as works of art those objects which **XI** evoke some emotion in their beholders, we have (Dentists' Drills) a similarly heterogeneous collection of stimulants, with no particular reason adduced why emotion is held to be desirable. If it is said that Art is what causes desirable emotions we find ourselves again in the familiar field of the moralist.

Without, however, bringing in moral considerations there are some emotions which have value, and which works of art can impart (Plate XI). It is clear that this view covers many works of a high order in which consistency of emotional sequence is the ruling principle.

Por linage de ebreos

Plate XI. See page 54

" He is gone on the mountain,
　　He is lost to the forest,
Like a summer-dried fountain,
　　When our need was the sorest.
The font, reappearing
　　From the raindrops shall borrow,
But to us comes no cheering,
　　To Duncan no morrow !

The hand of the reaper
　　Takes the ears that are hoary,
But the voice of the weeper
　　Wails manhood in glory.
The autumn winds rushing
　　Waft the leaves that are serest,
But our flower was in flushing,
　　When blighting was nearest.

Fleet foot on the correi,
　　Sage council in cumber,
Red hand in the foray,
　　How sound is thy slumber !
Like the dew on the mountain,
　　Like the foam on the river,
Like the bubble on the fountain,
　　Thou art gone, and for ever ! "

It will be admitted that emotional art merits the wide attention which it receives, and if (as in the case of Millet and Rembrandt, Tchaikowsky and Strauss) the emotions are refined and developed and general participation is made possible, it gains additional value.

But it is not easy to ascribe the highest value to emotions in general, merely as emotions. They may often be experienced without particular significance, and have their place without necessarily being the concern of art. For these reasons most writers who have advanced the emotionalist theory have felt constrained to narrow the field to **XII** some unique emotion. Introspective analysis, however, has not convinced psychologists that the postulated emotion can be admitted. It is not otherwise known, has never been described, and is much in need of identification.

XII.

SIGNIFICANT FORM

Failing some non-circular method of describing such an emotion, no field of inquiry emerges.* Some however of the incidental remarks by which this doctrine is supported in what is the best known of recent expositions deserve attention.

Mr. Clive Bell begins by defining " works of art " as " the objects that provoke a peculiar emotion (aesthetic emotion)." So far all is well. He poses next, as " the

---

*Attempts to bring order into our treatment of such elusive experiences as that of Beauty are always liable to misunderstanding, and to criticism by those who are suspicious of ' theory,' or concern themselves exclusively with appreciation or creative work. Sometimes this mistrust is due to a preference for 'evocative' language where questions of feeling and appreciation are concerned, and to this we refer later. But artists or musicians are also commonly supposed to resent what they regard as an endeavour to label, and by implication limit, the 'life of the spirit,'—to define, as the phrase goes, what is essentially 'indefinable.' To any such resentment we could only reply that it would have been based on a misinterpretation of our purpose. If what is regarded as the essential in such experiences seems neither to fall into one of the groups in which we have arranged the judgments of the past and of the present, nor to be covered by some obvious combination of these, nothing that is said here would conflict with the addition to the list of further descriptions. Even to those who doubt the possibility of an authentic description, the knowledge of what has actually been said or thought on any subject is seldom without value. And a conviction that the vocabulary of 'Pleasure' or 'Expression' or 'Emotion' is inadequate to the description sought may lead to the consideration of other mental states and to a better understanding of these—if not to the conclusion which is suggested below that the imagined *impasse* was due to a wrong orientation, rather than to the deficiencies of language or the baffling complexity of the subject.

central problem of aesthetics," the discovery of "some quality common and peculiar to all the objects that provoke this emotion." Now this, as our analysis will show, is a purely artificial question due to superstitions about causes and effects. No such common and peculiar quality can reasonably be looked for, if we start from Mr. Clive Bell's starting point. The "central problem" he proposes to solve does not arise.

His reason for this divagation is given on the same page ; "either all works of visual art have some common quality, or when we speak of 'works of art' we gibber." This is true, but the required quality is already to hand in his definition. When we speak of "works of art" we understand "objects which provoke aesthetic emotion." So far as this argument goes, there is no reason whatever to go seeking for further points of agreement.*

* But it may be said "If certain objects agree in producing in us a peculiar effect (aesthetic emotion) is not this fact a ground for supposing that there must be something common and peculiar in them to which this effect is due?" The plausibility of this fallacy is well known and it is clear that Mr. Clive Bell has been victimised. That it is a fallacy becomes plain when we consider a few analogous cases. Thus of all the things which cause death we can say if we like that they are lethal, but we are no longer tempted to think that we are saying anything more about them than that death did occur in connection with them. We no longer taboo them on the ground that they must necessarily have something deathly within them. Similarly with pleasing things, or with things which hurt, or with frightening things. More evidently still with beautiful things. The way in which the fallacy comes to seem plausible is best shown by taking a case in which we can make our statements

Which explains why Mr. Clive Bell's second
definition of Significant Form as "aesthetically

more precise. We may admit that things which hurt need
have no common quality, but still hold that if we narrow down
the kind of pain produced we shall be able then to find a common
peculiar quality in the things which cause it. Thus the pain
of being burnt we shall say implies heat and the pain of being
cut implies sharpness, and similarly the effect produced by a
work of art (aesthetic emotion) implies a common peculiar
quality in works of art.

But at this point in our narrowing down we automatically
beg the question. What we refer to by " the common peculiar
quality " is nothing different from the character of the effect
we notice. We are simply grammatically translating a description of an effect which we experience into a description of
the most prominent object connected with the effect. We do
not say any more by this procedure. "That causes me aesthetic
emotion " and " That has a peculiar quality such that I have
aesthetic emotion before it " are identical assertions, *if our sole
ground for the second is the first.* For purposes of writing
and speech the alternative locution is convenient when those
who use it know what they are doing. But we must be able to
distinguish the cases where we know independently both common
qualities of causes and common qualities of effects (and so can
set about observing their connections), from those cases where we
only know common qualities of effects and try from these to
infer common qualities in their causes. In the first case we have
something to investigate. In the second case we are limited to
grammatical tricks with our symbols.

If this point of view be accepted, and in addition if the search
for *'the* meaning of Beauty' be abandoned in favour of the
procedure here advocated, it will be clear that what is regarded
as important in one treatment may be neglected in another. It
follows, therefore, that though a philosopher or critic may have
been 'wrong' in the 'solution' he has put forward (the field
he has selected), he may, as we frequently have occasion to point
out, have made valuable remarks on matters which, for his purposes, appeared to be of secondary interest. And further verbal
differences, due to his philosophic system, may conceal a real
agreement, which translation or regrouping would serve to reveal.
The method of approach here employed is one which involves
certain deviations from accepted groupings and terminology ;
but that deviation is not such that intelligibility would be in-
creased by the creation of a new vocabulary, nor is it greater
than that caused in the case of others by their difference of out-
look, for which we have endeavoured, on all occasions, to allow.

moving form " has seemed to some people to carry the matter very little further ; and also why he sets out with such confidence to shew that what moves me, moves me, *i.e.*, " to show that significant form is the only quality common and peculiar to all the works of visual art that move me " (p. 10). He is too modest, however, in describing this arrangement of words as an hypothesis. There is no reason to suppose that there must be some one quality without which a work of art cannot exist (p. 7), particularly for an author who especially asserts (p. 8), that "we have no other means of recognizing a work of art than our feeling for it."

None the less, the phrase 'significant form' seems to exercise a hypnotic influence. Mr. Roger Fry, for example, whose earlier view, as published in the *New Quarterly* in 1909, was that Beauty is what arouses ordered emotion satisfying to the imaginative life (*i.e.*, a straightforward emotionalist theory of Type XI) is amongst those who have succumbed. In his recently published *Vision and Design* (p. 195) he says : " Some artists who were peculiarly sensitive to the formal relations of works of art had almost no sense of the emotions which I had supposed them to convey. . . It became evident that I had not pushed the analysis of works of art far enough." And he finally enumerates as amongst the questions of aesthetics which remain to be solved the nature of 'significant form,' and "what is the value of this elusive and—taking the whole mass of mankind—rather uncommon emotion which it causes." As in the case of his excursions into logic (" The specifically aesthetic emotion by means of which the necessity of relations is apprehended, and which corresponds in science to the purely logical process." *Athenæum*, 1919), Mr. Fry is unfortunate when he ceases to rely on his own judgment. The state of mind which he and Mr. Clive Bell discuss *may* be what will later be described* in connection with Synaesthesis, and, if so, we shall avoid the tacitly anti-Tolstoyan† view that Beauty is only for a select few who are endowed

---

* It is necessary to bear in mind the distinction between the evocative and the scientific use of language. Evocative language which is employed primarily to produce effects by suggestion, may (as is obvious in all poetry) be highly misleading if interpreted as though it had a scientific function. Thus the phrase 'Significant form,' meaningless if we ask logically 'significant of what ?' may be of value in giving the mind a certain direction, which may help to account for its appeal to certain readers.

† It is odd that Mr. Fry (p. 193) attaches so much importance to Tolstoi's least original tenet. That art is the *communication* of something may be regarded as common ground to all aesthetics (*cf.* even Coleridge's mockery of the novel : " A sort of mental *camera obscura* manufactured at the printing office, which *pro tempore* fixes, reflects, and transmits the moving phantasms of one man's delirium, so as to people the barrenness of a hundred other brains afflicted with the same trance."— *Biog. Lit.* chap. 3). Tolstoi's originality lay chiefly in his insistence on *universality* as a test of great art—the width of the appeal; he had no historical acquaintance with aesthetics, and relied chiefly on the paraphrases in Knight's uncritical compilation.

with the faculty of recognizing this esoteric entity.

"Lo in these hours supreme,
  No poem proud I chanting bring thee, nor
    mastery's rapturous verse,
  But a cluster containing night's darkness
    and blood-dripping wounds,
And psalms of the dead."

XIII.

EMPATHY

It remains conceivable, that a work of art should have some one quality in virtue of which we recognise it as such, though there are very strong general reasons against the assumption. It is plain that a description of what happens when we feel aesthetic emotion (if ever we do) would fall into two halves. There would be a long psychological story about the organisation of our impulses and instincts and of the special momentary setting of them due to our environment and our immediate past history on the one hand. On the other a physico-physiological account of the work of art as a stimulus, describing also its immediate sensory effects, and the impulses which these bring into play. The responsibility for the aesthetic emotion which results must be shared among all these factors. Even if we can detect some of the more important factors in the psychological conditions and group them as constant, as we seem to do when we talk of 'sensitive persons,' we are still left with a very complicated set of conditions.

" O gentle sleep !
Nature's soft nurse, how have I frighted thee,
That thou no more wilt weigh my eyelids
    down,
And steep my senses in forgetfulness ?
Why rather, sleep, liest thou in smoky cribs
Upon uneasy pallets stretching thee,
And hushed with buzzing night-flies to thy
    slumber,
Than in the perfumed chambers of the great,
Under the canopies of costly state,
And lulled with sounds of sweetest melody ?
O thou dull god !   Why liest thou with the vile,
In loathsome beds, and leav'st the kingly
    couch,
A watch-case, or a common 'larum bell?
Wilt thou upon the high and giddy mast
Seal up the ship-boy's eyes, and rock his
    brains
In cradle of the rude imperious surge,
And in the visitation of the winds,
Who take the ruffian billows by the top,
Curling their monstrous heads and hanging
    them
With deaf'ning clamours in the slippery
    clouds,
That, with the hurly, death itself awakes ?
Can'st thou, O partial sleep ! give thy repose
To the wet sea-boy in an hour so rude ;
And in the calmest and most stillest night,
With all appliances and means to boot,
Deny it to a king ? "

Plate XII.

See page 65

Let us but attempt to realise what is involved here! The likelihood that there is any one condition which is essential grows the smaller, the more we realise what the degree of this complexity must be. There is good reason to deny that emotion is ever the result of the stimulation merely of one impulse. It seems to be due always to the interaction of many. A long psychological investigation opens here. One branch of this explored with great care by Lipps, has in the natural course of such things been transformed into an aesthetic. This is **XIII**, Empathy.

It is well known that we are supposed to ascribe movement to lines and shapes which in themselves are essentially stationary, just as we ascribe body to pictorial surfaces. The doctrine of Einfühlung or Empathy advocated by Lipps, is an attempt to explain this phenomenon. Lotze in his *Mikrokosmos* remarked on the way in which we " project ourselves into the forms of a tree, identifying our life with that of the slender shoots which swell and stretch forth, feeling in our souls the delight of the branches which drop and poise delicately in mid-air. We extend equally to lifeless things these feelings which lend them meaning" (Plate XII). Almost any illustration from poetry will make this point plain. And by such feelings we transform the inert masses of a building into so many limbs of a living body, a body experiencing inner

E

strains which we transport back in ourselves. "We have," said Souriau (*Esthètique du Mouvement*, 1889) a quarter of a century later "only one way of imagining things from inside, and that is putting ourselves inside them."

Forms, says Lipps, arise in reality under specified mechanical conditions, to which we give the name of forces. What we call the rhythm of poetry again, is a rhythm of the acts of perceiving the accentuated and unaccentuated or less accentuated syllables. And since rhythm is universal in character, any psychical process can become the vehicle thereof, with a result that we get a sympathetic vibration of the whole personality, a connecting rhythm and mood.

> "And the invisible rain did ever sing
> A silver music on the mossy lawn."

So the qualities which we attribute (as we attribute to other things frightfulness, novelty and quaintness) to rhythms, sounds and colours (seriousness and cheerfulness : fullness and quietness : warmth and depth) are not heard and seen, but denote the manner in which we are internally moved when sounds and colours are being perceived.

> "The pillowy silkiness that rests
> Full in the speculation of the stars."

Aesthetic pleasure, Lipps concluded is " dependent upon the attribution of life," and aesthetic contemplation always involves such attributes. Space, for example, is an object of aesthetic perception "only inasmuch as it is a space which has been given life," and is thus the vehicle of inner tension ; and it is the mission of the arts of beautiful spatial form to increase this interchange of activities and to diversify it. Here, with the addition of a few stray dicta about ' meaningful rhythms of living,' Lipps concludes his account, leaving it to others to develop out of such considerations any more definite approximation to an aesthetic. And independently, or under the influence of his analysis, these others have not been wanting.*

The only reason which prevents such accounts of empathic processes being formulated as a complete aesthetic theory, is the uncertainty of their authors as to what sort of answers may be expected to the question

* Says Berenson *Tuscan Painters*, p. 84, " The more we endow an object with human attributes, the less we merely know, and the more we realise it, the more does it approach the work of art," and we find those who approach the same question from the standpoint of psychological theory finding the whole solution in the field of empathic processes. " If the energies which we feel in the lines are external projections of our own energies," says Münsterberg, " we understand the psychological reasons why certain combinations of lines please us and others do not. They ought to be such that they correspond to the natural energies of our own organism and represent the harmony of our own muscular functions."

"What is Beauty?" For all these accounts introduce at the critical point some implication as to 'pleasure' or 'harmony' or to both of these, in such a way as to leave it open whether their discussion has not merely been concerned with a part of the machinery of appreciation in general.

Vernon Lee's elaborate summary of the whole controversy is at once the clearest indication of this uncertainty, and the most confused in its ultimate conclusions. Referring to the place of memory in the story, she remarks (*Beauty and Ugliness*, p. 21) :—
"The projection of an experience into the non-ego involves the more or less vivid revival of that experience in ourselves ; and that revival, according to its degree of vividness, is subject to the same accompaniment of satisfaction or dissatisfaction as the original experience. So when this attribution of our modes of life to visible shapes and this revival of past experience is such as to be favourable to our existence and in so far pleasurable, we welcome the form thus animated by ourselves as 'beautiful.'" Hence, she concludes, "Empathy has conditioned the being of art and can explain it." We could hardly ask more of a Theory of Beauty. We have, it appears, a defining judgment to enable us to distinguish which projections are beautiful, and an account of projections and their stimulation which enables us to

Plate XIII.

See page 69

differentiate the class of objects that can act as stimuli.

Thus :—

1. Not all objects, but those into which we can project movement correlated with a peculiar dynamical experience in ourselves, are aesthetic.

2. Not all such objects are beautiful, but those which cause pleasure, because they facilitate our vitality (*cf.* Plate XIII).

"I hear a springing water, whose quick sound
Makes softer the soft sunless patient air."

In the light of our previous remarks, however, the claim has only to be stated for its weakness to become apparent. In the first place, unless it is deliberately to be interpreted as differing from the doctrine of pleasure, we have merely that doctrine stated in a vaguer form and over a more limited range. Secondly, the experiences we get from successfully riding a bicycle, which presumably cause pleasure and facilitate our vitality, could clearly be recalled by our projecting similar movements into lines and rhythms, and the resultant state would be neither more nor less aesthetic than the original one, except in virtue of its new origin in recall through projection. And such an origin is hardly more relevant to aesthetics than if the same state were to be recalled by internal stimuli in a dream.

This does not mean that it would be impossible to find fields which on such principles could be labelled 'Aesthetics' by an enthusiastic empathist *pur sang*, but since no one not misled by terminology has yet marked out such a field *qua* aesthetician, it is hardly worth while to set up and overturn dummies for hypothetical monomaniacs.

As regards the general nature of Empathy as part of the process of appreciation, we may note that the terminology in which it has been described has itself misled even the ablest writers on the subject. The treachery of the term *Einfühlung*, as used by Professor Lipps, has been well indicated by Vernon Lee. In its reflexive form it implies that the ego or *personality* in some sense goes over into the object, and is merged therein, so that Lipps contended that if Empathy was in progress, we could not be aware of the inner imitation or muscular movements which (in the similar view of Groos) accompany the process.

The importance of this sort of consideration lies in its bearing on the " impersonal " attitude which is regarded by many as the essential of aesthetic contemplation.

Whatever the importance of empathic phenomena when correctly described in shewing us how we come to speak of certain objects as we do, it should be clear that they do not provide a consistent theory of Beauty in the same way that the hedonic theory does ; though an empathic theory has been verbally formulated by some of its advocates so as to lead them to suppose that an aesthetic had been involved. Moreover, there is undoubtedly a sense in which certain relations of formal symmetry, a certain distribution of weight, the even interplay of qualities and intensities, may lead to a mere judgment of balance on the perceptual level, the balance being usually judged to be in the work of art. Where undue importance is claimed for this type of judgment, inadequate theories tend to arise, which narrow the application of the term balance, although such superficial balances may create a predisposition towards the more important forms of appreciation with which we are about to deal.

Throughout the discussion of empathy, with its account of the initiation of impulses, and its glances at the physiology and psychology of certain elementary forms of balance we find ourselves constantly approaching or entering the field which our enquiry had reached when the claims of the emotionalist had engaged attention.

XIV.

SYNAESTHESIS

It remains only to formulate **XVI** a doctrine which seems essentially that to be attributed to Confucius in the quotations from the Chung Yung at the head of this article. In doing so we shall be enabled to place in their true position the two remaining definitions on our list. It is expected that the experience now about to be described will be recognised by those who look for it; it has, indeed, been noticed by many poets and critics. It marks off a field which cannot otherwise be defined and also explains why the objects therein contained can reasonably be regarded as of great importance. The limits of this field do not correspond with those set by a naive use of the term Beauty, but it will be found that the actual usage of careful and sensitive persons not affected by special theories corresponds as closely with this definition as with any other which can be given.

"And when there came a pause
Of silence such as baffled his best skill :
Then sometimes, in that silence, while he hung
Listening, a gentle shock of mild surprise
Has carried far into his heart the voice
Of mountain torrents ; or the visible scene
Would enter unawares into his mind
With all its solemn imagery, its rocks,
Its woods, and that uncertain heaven received
Into the bosom of the steady lake."

The experience though fugitive and evanescent in the extreme may yet be analysed by a consideration of the occasions on which we became aware of it in a more gradual manner. Limiting ourselves for the moment to the visual field we are aware of certain shapes and colours. These when more closely studied usually reveal themselves as in three dimensions, or as artists say, in forms. These forms must in some cases, but in others may not, be identified as this or that physical object. Throughout this process impulses are aroused and sustained, which gradually increase in variety and degree of systematisation. To these systems in their early stages will correspond the emotions such as joy, horror, melancholy, anger, and mirth; or attitudes, such as love, veneration, sentimentality. Songs like this are written:

" Break, break, break,
    On thy cold gray stones, O Sea !
And I would that my tongue could utter
    The thoughts that arise in me.

O well for the fisherman's boy
    That he shouts with his sister at play!
O well for the sailor lad,
    That he sings in his boat on the bay !

And the stately ships go on
    To their haven under the hill ;
But O for the touch of a vanished hand,
    And the sound of a voice that is still !"

In the interpretation of works of art at an early stage, if we allow ourselves to take on the appropriate mood, we may **XV** come into contact with the personality of the artist.

What he puts into his work is a selection made from an indefinitely large number of possible elements, and their specific arrangement is also only one of many possible. This selection and arrangement is due to the direction and accentuation of his interest— in other words to the play of impulses which controls his activity at the moment ; and it is often such that the same group of impulses are aroused in the spectator. We do not make the artist's selection because that is done for us. This seems to be the only way, unless by telepathy, of coming into contact with other minds than our own. Some rest content with this contact, which is plainly a matter of degree.

So far, however, we need not have experienced Beauty, but it is here that our emotion assumes a more general character, and we find that correspondingly our attitude has become impersonal. The explanation of this change is of the greatest importance. The various impulses before alluded to have become further systematised and intensified. Not all impulses, it is plain, as usually excited, are naturally harmonious, for conflict is possible and common. A complete systematisation must take the form of such an adjustment as will preserve free play to every impulse, with entire avoidance of frustration. In any equilibrium of this kind, however momentary, (*cf. Frontispiece*) we are experiencing beauty.

The state of equilibrium is not one of passivity, inertia, over-stimulation or conflict, and most people would be rightly dissatisfied with such terms as Nirvana, Ecstasy, Sublimation or At-oneness with Nature*, which might at first sight be thought appropriate. As descriptive of an aesthetic state in which impulses are experienced *together*, the word

* " La beauté anésthetique de la nature," says Lalo (*Introduction à l'Esthétique*, p. 146) " c'est une sympathie universelle pour la vie et l'être quels qu'ils soient, c'est une intuition panthéistique de la solidarité foncière de toutes choses, ou, si l'on veut, c'est le sentiment de la nature : de toute la nature, sans choix aucun, du moins en principe; et non de la 'belle nature.'"

(Plate I).

Synaesthesis, however, conveniently covers both equilibrium and harmony. The whole subject of Harmony as distinct from Equilibrium requires as careful a treatment, which is attempted by the same authors elsewhere.*

In equilibrium, there is no tendency to action, and any concert-goer must have realised the impropriety of the view that action is the proper outcome of aesthetic appreciation.

---

* *Colour-Harmony* (Kegan Paul 1922). It is, perhaps, worth while to note that the frequent use of the word Harmony to characterise various mental states felt to be valuable, both by those who aspire to be " in tune with the Infinite," and by writers on art generally, does not necessarily imply anything in common with that intended here. For example : " Man is supremely conscious of a dualism within himself—of a war in his members which a higher spiritual harmony alone can quell." (*Hermaia* : Comparative Aesthetics by Colin McAlpin, p. 363). The dualism is essentially that of Kant or Schiller, if not of Plato's steeds; and similarly when, in the course of her remarks on Empathy Vernon Lee quotes Fräulein von Ritóok, " Harmony is the empathic unity of the psychical experience," and adds " the microcosm asserts itself with its insistence on plan, unity, harmony . . . . Art would, therefore, be a school for this unity of mood, purpose, and plan, without which consciousness would disintegrate and human life disappear . . . . The unethical, the unintellectual man, like the unaesthetic is the one who is in conflict with himself," the relation to what has been said above may be chiefly verbal. At first sight more hesitation might be felt with the *obiter dicta* of the eclectic Paul Gaultier who, in his *Meaning of Art* (trans. 1913) speaks, p. 25, of " the harmonious and integral expansion of all our nature in the function of feeling," and describes ugliness (p. 59) as " a rupture of equilibrium, the disorganisation of a whole, the result of a conflict of active finalities, which in spite of their opposition are, nevertheless, each for itself elements of harmony." When, however, Gaultier asks (p. 29), " Is not aesthetic emotion fundamentally creative of harmony ? " and speaks (p. 136) of this emotion making us " unite our voice in the melody and our active movements with music or the dance," we can answer that, as we have endeavoured to shew, harmony in this sense is a very different thing from equilibrium.

When impulses are 'harmonised' on the other hand they work together, and such disciplined co-ordination in action is much to be desired in other places. When works of art produce such action, or conditions which lead to action, they have either not completely fulfilled their function or would in the view of equilibrium here being considered be called not ' beautiful ' but 'stimulative.'*

*Although the experience here described is readily recognisable, this account is admittedly speculative. The argumentative will need no prompting to the remark that the distinction between a balance and a deadlock is difficult to explain. Two particular cases which may produce misapprehension are worth noting.

The first is the case of irresolution. It may be supposed that here we have a balance of impulses by which we seem to be impelled first one way and then another with too rapid an alternation or too weak a thrust for either impulse to take effect. This condition must be marked off as totally distinct from that which we describe as equilibrium. The difference between them is theoretically as follows. In an equilibrium the impulses active, however they are specifically related, do yet sustain one state of mind. They combine to produce one phase of consciousness. In irresolution the sets of impulses sustain severally their independent phases. In some cases, what is essentially an oscillation may become a balance. The difference may be found in the cross connections between the subsidiary impulses contained in these oscillating systems. Two perfectly simple impulses, we may suppose, must either oscillate or lock. A more complex initial conflict may on the other hand discharge itself through its branch connections. We might describe balance as a conflict of impulses solving itself in the arousal of the other impulses of the personality. Balance as we have said above tends to bring the whole of the personality into play.

The other confusing case is that in which no conflict arises because only one self-sufficing set of impulses is in action. The state of mind which then arises seems in many ways to resemble balance. In intense anger or joy for instance, we have a certain lucidity, self-possession and freedom which might be mistaken for some of the conditions which arise in balance. But the resemblances are illusory as time shows. Balance refreshes and never exhausts.

As we realise beauty we become more fully ourselves the more our impulses are engaged. If, as is sometimes alleged, we are the whole complex of our impulses, this fact would explain itself. Our interest is not canalised in one direction rather than another. It becomes ready instead to take any direction we choose. This is the explanation of that detachment so often mentioned in artistic experience.* We become impersonal or disinterested.

"Yet once more, O ye Laurels, and once more
Ye Myrtles brown, with Ivy never-sear,
I com to pluck your Berries harsh and crude,
And with forc'd fingers rude,
Shatter your leaves before the mellowing year."

* In this context the view of those modern psychologists who, like Münsterberg, regard Beauty as an experience of unity projected ("So far as this will is projected into the drama itself, its unity gives us the aesthetic value of a work of art"—"Music forms an inner world to a unified tissue of volitions." *The Eternal Values* pp. 200, 252), and occasionally treat this 'unity' as equivalent to 'harmony' (*Ibid.*, p. 202), may be contrasted with the following account of Cézanne's attitude—

"L'art est une harmonie parallèle à la nature. Que penser des imbéciles qui vous disent: le peintre is toujours inférieur à la nature! Il lui est parallèle. S'il n' intervient pas volontairement . . . entendez moi bien. Toute sa volonté doit être de silence. Il doit faire taire en lui toutes les voix préjugés, oublier, oublier, faire silence, être un écho parfait. Alors sur sa plaque sensible, tout le paysage s'inscrira. Pour le fixer sur la toile, l'extérioriser, le métier interviendra ensuite, mais le métier respectueux qui, lui aussi, n' est prêt qu' à obéir, à traduire inconsciemment, tant il sait bien sa langue, le texte qu'il déchiffre, les deux textes parallèles, la nature vive, la nature senti, celle qui est là . . . (*il montrait la plaine verte et bleue*) celle qui est ici (*il se frappait le front*) qui toutes deux doivent s'amalgamer pour durer."—Joachim Gasquet, *Cézanne*, p. 81.

78

Simultaneously, as another aspect of the same adjustment, our individuality becomes differentiated or isolated from the individualities of things around us. We become less ' mixed into ' other things. As we become more ourselves they become more themselves, because we are less dependent upon the particular impulses which they each arouse in us.

As a corollary of this individualisation, particular sets of impulses are felt in relation to other sets, which, unless both were already active in the equilibrium, would not occur.*

*The following quotation may serve as an illustration:—

" 'Well, and what then ? You have known a *There* and a *Someone*. The *There* is the future life, the *Someone* is God.'

Prince André did not reply. The carriage and horses had long been led out on to the further bank, and were already harnessed ; the sun was half-sunken beneath the horizon, and the evening frost was beginning to encrust the little pools by the shore with starry crystals, while Pierre and André, to the astonishment of the servants, coachmen and ferryman, still stood in the boat talking.

' If God and the future life exist, then truth and virtue exist ; and man's highest happiness consists in striving for their attainment. One must live,' said Pierre, ' one must love, one must believe that we live, not merely now on this patch of earth, but that we have lived and shall live eternally there in the universe.' He pointed to the sky.

Prince André stood leaning on the rail of the ferry-boat, and listening to Pierre. He never moved his eyes, but gazed at the red reflection of the sun in the dark-blue flood. Pierre ceased speaking. All was silent. The ferry-boat lay drifted along the bank, and only the ripples of the current could be heard lapping feebly against its sides. Prince André fancied that this patter of the water babbled a refrain to Pierre's words, ' That is sooth, accept it : that is sooth, accept it.' "

EDUCATION.

The educative value of art derives partly from this heightened power of differentiation and partly also from the sympathetic understanding of other personalities discussed under the heading of contact above. Art is a means of establishing relations with personalities not otherwise accessible. The gulf which separates us from ancient peoples, savages, enemies, allies, people of another sex, children, or the aged is thus bridged (Plate XIV). The exertions of the majority of anthropologists might have been more valuable had they not shown themselves unable or unwilling to use this obvious method of understanding.

UN PAPILLON (parle).

"Mes ailes sont douces comme de la poussière de velours. Je suis tout étonné de vivre. Je ne comprends pas grand'chose, mais je suis beau. Le pluie facilement déchirerait mon aile rouge et noire qui bat lourdement sur mes pattes."

Such differences as do occur in the experience we feel as an intensification, a broadening or a deepening of the mood, and may be probably due to the range of impulses involved and their movement about a centre. We experience it under widely different circumstances and in connexion with widely different

Plate XIV.

See page 80

objects not usually considered under categories of art ; for instance in the performance of a scientific operation, in the regulation of conduct, or indeed in connexion with any natural or imagined object. Descriptions by the poets are abundant.

EARLY SPECULATIONS

Early speculations on the subject of aesthetics were too preoccupied with religious and metaphysical issues to allow any clear statement in this field. Intellectualist theories occasionally allude to harmonious activity. Thus Kant* speaks of " a reciprocal subjective common accord of the power of cognition. . . The quickening of both faculties (imagination and understanding) to an indefinite but yet, thanks to the given representation, harmonious activity is the sensation whose universal communicability is postulated by the judgment of taste." And it was Kant's view of the relations of Art and Play which led Schiller in his *Briefe über die ästhetische Erziehung des Menschen* to elaborate a theory of harmonious activity in which a balance or equipoise is maintained.

There are, according to Schiller (Letter 2.), two opposing demands in man—that of the sense-impulse, and that of the form-impulse. Whenever the form-impulse prevails (Letter 12) " there is the highest amplitude of being."

* *Critique of Aesthetic Judgement*, trans. Meredith, pp. 59-60.

F

But if we subordinate (Letter 13) the sensuous to the rational, we get mere antagonism and no harmony. Harmony can be attained without diminution of either. And here the function of Play is introduced.

The object of the sense-impulse is *life*, the object of the form-impulse *shape* (Letter 15). The object of the play-impulse, expressed in a general proposition, can then be called *living shape*, or in its widest signification, Beauty. Beauty, then (Letter 16), results from the reciprocity of two opposite impulses, and from the union of the opposite principles ; we must seek its highest ideal in the most perfect possible *equipoise*.

" The scales of a balance stand poised," he proceeds (Letter 20) " when they are empty ; but also when they contain equal weights. Thus the mind passes from perception to reflection by an intermediate state (*Stimmung*) in which sense and reason are active at the same time, but thus mutually destroy their determining power and effect a negation through an opposition . . . if we call the condition of sensuous determination the physical, and that of reflective determination the logical and moral condition, we must call the condition of real and active determinableness the aesthetic condition." And again, when a thing relates " to the entirety of our different powers, without being a definite object to any single one of them—that is its *aesthetic* character."

It will be evident that, as in the case of Kant, the formulation of an aesthetic theory in terms of sense and reason, life and shape, cannot be satisfactory. The ambiguity of such terms makes it doubtful whether Schiller is not describing an ordinary balanced mind of the Aristotelian type. It is easy to describe in haste the experience of Beauty in a way which makes it closely resemble either mystical states, or a mere level-headed alertness, or some form of self-contained and controlled sensibility.

"What rigorous calm! What almost holy silence!
　　All the doors are shut, and the beds of flowers
　　are giving out scent; discreetly, of course...

Two women that lean against each other, stand to the balustrade of red marble on the edge of the terrace.

One of them wishes to speak, to confide to her friend the secret sorrow that is agonizing her heart.

She throws an anxious glance at the motionless leaves,
　　and because of a paroquet with iridescent wings
　　that perches on a branch, she sighs and is silent."

If too simple a view of balance be taken the theory we are describing approximates to a recipe. Is it not possible that Gœthe may have acted on some such recipe in the construction of *Faust* and *Wilhelm Meister ?* In any case the conception of a dual opposition is over-simple, and as Schiller's account which follows would suggest, fails to provide any adequate explanation of the experience he himself describes. The experience of Beauty, he continues (Letter 21), gives us no particular sort of knowledge and has no direct utility, but renders it possible for a man " to make out of himself what he will, and restores to him the freedom to be what he ought to be." At the moment, when we are enjoying Beauty (Letter 22) we are "equally master of our passive and active powers, and with equal facility do we address ourselves to the serious and to sport, to calm and to emotion, to compliance and to resistance, to abstract reflection and to intuition. It is in this state of equanimity and freedom of spirit, united with power and activity, that a genuine work of art should leave us. If, after an enjoyment of this kind we find ourselves predisposed to some one particular mode of feeling or action, unfit for and averse to another," we have, according to Schiller, a certain proof that a purely aesthetic state has not been reached. The following passage from *Resurrection* raises this problem:—

"But here her cry was suddenly changed to moaning, and then died down entirely. One of the attendants caught hold of her arms, which he bound, and the other gagged her with a piece of cloth, which he tied behind her head, so that she might not be able to tear it off.

She looked at the attendants and at the officer with eyes bulging out of their orbits, her whole face jerked, a noisy breath issued from her nose, and her shoulders rose up to her ears and fell again.

'You must not make such a scandal,—I told you so before. It is your own fault,' said the officer, going out.

The chimes played in a soft tone, 'How glorious is our Lord in Zion.' The sentries were changed. In the cathedral candles burned, and a sentry stood at the tombs of the Tsars."

Schiller held that no work of art is in reality purely aesthetic, believing that we are not completely prepared for "abstract reflection directly after lofty musical enjoyment"; though the more universal the medium and the art, the nearer its approximation to the ideal. And, as regards subject, "true æsthetic freedom is to be expected only from form . . . and the more imposing and attractive the subject is in itself, or the more inclined the observer is to merge himself immediately in the subject, the more triumphant is the art which overcomes the former and maintains authority over the latter."

MODERN PSYCHOLOGY

It is surprising that, whatever its value, Schiller's theory has not attracted more attention. In Germany it seems to have been absorbed into metaphysical speculations such as those of Schelling, but of recent years it finds a place in the writings of Waldemar Conrad (*Zeitschrift für Aesthetik*, 1912), who related it to the educational ideals of Herbart. Modern psychologists have, in fact, been curiously remiss in this respect with the notable exception of Miss Ethel D. Puffer, who, apparently overlooking Schiller's view, advances a somewhat similar account. At page 50 of her *Psychology of Beauty* we read :

" The psychological organism is in a state of unity either when it is in a state of virtual congealment or emptiness, as in a trance or ecstacy ; or when it is in a state of repose, without tendency to change. . . The only aesthetic repose is that in which stimulation resulting in impulse or movement is checked by its antagonistic impulse, combined with heightening of tone. But this is *tension, equilibrium,* or *balance of forces,* which is thus seen to be a general condition of all aesthetic experience."

The reference to "*its* antagonistic impulse," and "a general *condition*" are unconvincing ; and when Miss Puffer goes on to say that "the concept is familiar in pictorial composition," and adds (p. 125) that it is not beauty we seek from Hogarth and Goya, it is clear that she expects always to find the cause of balance in the construction of the work of art. Thus she quotes in favour of her view of Goya the following striking extract from Klinger on the subject of ' background ' : "Such a tone is the foil for psychological moments, as they are handled by Goya, for instance, with barbarically magnificent nakedness. On a background which is merely indicated, with few strokes which hardly indicate space, he impales like a butterfly the human type, mostly in a moment of folly or wickedness," which does as much as any description can to shew the kind of beauty Goya realised—a beauty obviously not of the objective (formal) kind which is all she is able to admit in satirical work. All through her treatment this assumption of an objective balance is in evidence, culminating in the final chapter, where (p. 279) a relapse into emotional expressionism occurs, in an attempt to discover such objective balance in moral ideas. The essential criticism of such an attempt is that an objective balance, as we have already stated, may indeed predispose to, but is not necessarily followed by, equilibrium ; and, further, this objective balance must be capable of being independently ascertained, not merely inferred from a subjective state.*

" I there before thee, in the country that well
>   thou knowest,
>   Already arrived am inhaling the odorous
>   air :
> I watch thee enter unerringly where thou
>   goest,
>   And anchor queen of the strange shipping
>   there,
>   Thy sails for awnings spread, thy masts
>   bare ;
> Nor is ought from the foaming reef to the
>   snow-capp'd, grandest
>   Peak, that is over the feathery palms
>   more fair
> Than thou, so upright, so stately, and still
>   thou standest."†

* It is a pity that so interesting a study should have so chaotic a conclusion. What, for example, is to be understood by the following remarks ? —
" That part of the effect of beauty in a picture which is due to the idea is thus the fundamental but merely abstract element of unity, contributing to the complex aesthetic state only the simplest condition (p. 279). . . Such specific emotion as may be detected in any aesthetic experience is, then, covered by the definition of beauty only in so far as it has become form rather than content—is valuable only in its relations rather than in itself (p. 283)."

† Contrast the following by the same writer for formal balance *without* synaesthesis.
>   "Thou, careless, awake !
>   Thou peacemaker, fight !
>   Stand England for honour
>   And God guard the Right ! " etc.

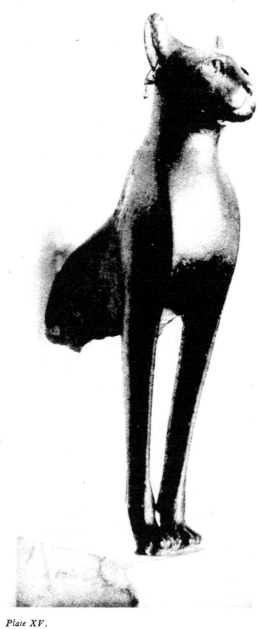

Plate XV.   See page 89

A more solid and satisfactory adaptation of this theory of equilibrium to the modern psychology of appreciation may be found in W. M. Urban's *Valuation* (p. 219), where it appears as "the concept of the widened ground of diffused stimulation, the *balance* of impulses, so that no one shall constitute an illusion-disturbing moment and lead to readjustment in a new value-movement; the consequent *repose* of emotion in the object and the *expansion* of feeling which goes with it. The ordering, rearrangement of content characteristic of the aesthetic experience is, therefore, in the service of the deepening, or enhancement of that fundamental mode of worth experience which is appreciatively described as the immanental reference." *And, again, in primitive dances the object of desire, whether martial, erotic or religious is "distanced,"† and "the fundamental conation becomes dispositional. This rhythm, usually

* This enhancement must not be confused with intensity or height of vitality. It is often suggested that **XIV** heightening vitality, which is usually an important accompaniment of the appreciation of good work (*cf*. Plate XV), is the chief aim of art. It may be readily admitted that mental and physical fitness is closely allied to equilibrium, but although equilibrium certainly conduces to health (promotes, *e.g.*, the circulation of the blood, and raises the general tone of the body), and health facilitates equilibrium, yet this is no reason for confusing the functions of the Studio and the Gymnasium.

†A development of this view of distance will be found in Mr. E. Bullough's article on 'Psychical distance' in the *British Journal of Psychology* (1912-13, p. 87). Such 'distancing' would, however, on any interpretation seem to be far from essential in the description of aesthetic experience.

of the form of advance or retreat, of affirmation and arrest of expression, produces an equilibrium of impulses, which prevents the fundamental tendency from breaking forth into overt action."

It might be assumed from these quotations that Urban's account is identical with that which we have given above, but this is by no means the case, for his masterly systematisation has the defects of its qualities. In the process of erecting his monumental edifice, he has sometimes been led to build with material of imperfect homogeneity, and has consequently incorporated in the fabric elements which are essentially disruptive. Combined with his analysis of the equilibration of impulses are importations from the systems of Marshall* and Groos, which falsify the description of the way in which equilibrium is brought about. In particular, the constant reference to " illusion-disturbing moments," in accordance with the theory of Groos that the elimination of these disturbing moments is necessary to the "Æsthetic illusion," vitiates the account of the balance which it is supposed to explain.

*Marshall, both in his *Aesthetic Principles*, p. 186, and *Pain, Pleasure and Aesthetics*, p. 332, is led by his hedonic assumptions to construct elaborate hypotheses as to the way in which the artist succeeds in 'widening' and giving permanence to the pleasures he is supposed to be concerned with. Such constructions cannot be profitably incorporated in an account so differently orientated as the above.

CONCLUSION

In conclusion, the reason why equilibrium is a justification for the preference of one experience before another, is the fact that it brings into play all our faculties. In virtue of what we have called the synaesthetic character of the experience, we are enabled, as we have seen (p. 79) to appreciate relationships in a way which would not be possible under normal circumstances. Through no other experience can the full richness and complexity of our environment be realised. The ultimate value of equilibrium is that it is better to be fully than partially alive.

THE FOUNDATIONS OF AESTHETICS

W HEN *we have intelligence resulting from sincerity this condition is to be ascribed to nature ; when we have sincerity resulting from intelligence, this condition is to be ascribed to instruction. But given the sincerity and there shall be the intelligence ; given the intelligence and there shall be the sincerity.*

To this attainment there are requisite the extensive study of what is excellent, accurate enquiry about it, careful reflection on it, the clear discrimination of it, and the earnest practise of it.

Let a man proceed in this way and though dull he will surely become intelligent; though weak, he will surely become strong.

From the Chung Yung
The Doctrine of Equilibrium and Harmony

INDEX

INDEX

PASSAGES QUOTED